dabblelab

BUILD BUZZ-WORTHY VIDEO BLOGS

4D An Augmented Reading Experience

by Thomas Kingsley Troupe

Consultant:
Diana L. Rendina, MLIS
Media Specialist, Speaker, Writer
Tampa, FL

CAPSTONE PRESS
a capstone imprint

1 Ask an adult to download the app.  Capstone 4D Education

2 Scan any page with the star.

3 Enjoy your cool stuff!

— OR —

Use this password at capstone4D.com

videoblogs.40109

Dabble Lab Books are published by Capstone Press
1710 Roe Crest Drive
North Mankato, Minnesota 56003
www.mycapstone.com

Library of Congress Cataloging-in-Publication Data
Names: Troupe, Thomas Kingsley, author.
ISBN 978-1-5435-4010-9 (hardcover) | ISBN 978-1-5435-4018-5 (eBook PDF)

Editorial Credits
Shelly Lyons, editor; Sarah Bennett, designer; Morgan Walters, media researcher;
Katy LaVigne, production specialist

Photo Credits
iStockphoto: mustafagull, 10; Shutterstock: Artazum, top 21, Astarina, (action) Cover, Becris, (film) design element, Birdman Music, Audio file, Carla Nichiata, bottom 21, clickyusho.id, (clock) design element, Darcraft, (rec) Cover, Dmytro Zinkevych, 4, 5, glenda, left 13, Halfpoint, 12, katarina_1, (card) design element, Keep Calm and Vector, (sticker) design element, Lapina, (boys) Cover, top 13, Lightspring, background 45, Natasha Pankina, (icons) Cover, design element, ONYXprj, (laptop) Cover, Cover, design element throughout, photolinc, (watercolor) design element throughout, Redcollegiya, (cupcake) design element, Ryan DeBerardinis, top right 31, Seth Gallmeyer, (notebook) design element, Shorena Tedliashvili, (film strip) design element throughout, silm, (sketch notebook) design element, Vissay, (poster) bottom 45, Vyacheslav Sakhatsky, (camera) design element, weikwang, (muffine wrapper) design element

All internet sites, apps, and software programs appearing in back matter were available and accurate when this book was sent to press.

Printed and bound in China.
1671

CONTENTS

What's a Vlog?

A friendly face appears on your screen and starts to tell you about her day. She talks about a movie she's seen or a tasty lunch she's just eaten. A week later, the same person talks about her experience at a local store. Is this some kind of news show? Not really. It's a video blog! Video blogs (or vlogs) are videos people make of themselves to share thoughts, opinions, and experiences with viewers.

Video Blog Success Guide

Keep It Simple Don't overdo it with visual effects or weird, random noises. Your content should be exciting and interesting enough to hold the attention of your viewers without having to resort to cringe-worthy antics.

Take Your Time Don't be afraid to reshoot pieces of video if you don't like something. If you plan on sharing your video with the world, you should do it right!

Be Yourself A lot of YouTube or video blog "celebrities" try to put on a performance or act like someone they're not to generate followers. Break from the pack by being yourself! Acting too over-the-top and copying someone else's style is a recipe for disaster.

What You'll Need

☆ an idea
☆ an outline
☆ talent/you/guests
☆ a video camera/smartphone/ tablet
☆ a location
☆ lights
☆ a tripod
☆ editing software

Finding Gear

Video blogging shouldn't cost you a lot of money. Most likely, you can find what you need around your own home. Sure, many famous video bloggers use expensive gear, but that doesn't mean you need to. What really matters is coming up with interesting content. If you've got that, people will watch what you're doing!

Camera Ready

Digital Camera

One of the most important elements in making your video blog will be the camera. Find a digital camera that is simple to use and able to record long shots of video. You'll be taking lots of shots of yourself and your surroundings, so make sure the camera's memory card has space on it.

Smartphones and Tablets

If you can use a smartphone or tablet as your camera, you're in luck. Not only are smartphones small and easy to use, many of them have built-in video-editing apps. If yours doesn't, you can always add one. Be sure to have an adult help you download the app you need. As with a digital camera, make sure there's enough memory available for all the footage you'll shoot.

Webcam

Do you have a laptop or a personal computer? Chances are, it comes with a webcam already built in. While it's trickier to place the camera where you need it, you'll be able to see yourself as you're recording. If your computer doesn't have a webcam, you can find an inexpensive one pretty easily.

Action/GoPro Cameras

Using an action camera is another option. These little guys are great for doing video blogs on the go. They're sturdy and small enough to attach almost anywhere. Be sure you use one that is able to record sound. Some of them are video only.

Lights

Light! Use a lot of it. Your viewers need to see you or whatever it is you're trying to show them. If you use too little light, your image will look grainy.

Use overhead lights, lamps, or even natural light from a window. Take a couple sample shots and then review the footage to see what you think. If it's too bright, remove one light.

PRO TIP

Don't shoot video of yourself with your back to a bright, open window. You'll end up looking like a shadow, and people won't be able to see your face. Instead, turn and face the window and use that natural light.

Tripods

Planning on mostly sitting and talking to the camera during your video blog? Use a tripod. A tripod will keep your camera in place and leave your hands free. You can easily find one that will work fine for very little money.

Don't feel like you HAVE to use a tripod, though. If you're shooting your video blog on the go, you can always go "handheld." Just make sure you keep yourself or whatever you're filming as steady as possible. You don't want the shots to be too shaky.

phone tripod →

PRO TIP

Don't have a tripod? Use heavy objects like books to keep your camera secure and locked into place.

11

Ideas

The most difficult part of creating your own video blog is coming up with a good idea. Content is what the focus of your vlog is all about. What do you want to talk about? What would your viewers like to see? Be sure to ask friends and classmates what sort of videos they like to watch.

While there are no rules to what your video blog needs to be, it's good to find something you're passionate about. Do you like talking about movies? Vlog about it! Are you a big fan of video games? Talk about the game you're playing. Do a review!

Welcome to "Awesome Eats" with Jake and Travis.

I'm going to teach sports tips in my vlog!

PRO TIP

Be careful not to say things that could be hurtful to others. And don't call out people by name, unless you have their permission. Keep the focus on YOU and your likes and interests.

Planning Makes Perfect!

Schedule

A lot of popular online video bloggers (YouTubers) make frequent videos. They let their audience or followers know when they can expect to see something new from them. Some will even post a new video a few times a week.

What's your video blogging plan? Does your idea sound like it could be an ongoing thing? If so, plan out a handful of ideas and topics for future videos.

PRO TIP

You can lure in people to watch your next video by giving them a taste or "tease" of what you'll be doing next!

SUNDAY	MONDAY
31 BRAINSTORM Topics for the Month	**1** Create Outline
7	**8** Create Outline
14	**15** Create Outline
21	**22** Create Outline
28	**29**

TUESDAY	WEDNESDAY	THURSDAY	FRIDAY	SATURDAY
2 Prep for Shooting	3 Shooting Day!	4 Edit Video	5 Reshoot and Edit Video	6 Post Video
9 Prep for Shooting	10 Shooting Day!	11 Edit Video	12 Reshoot and Edit Video	13 Post Video
16 Prep for Shooting	17 Shooting Day!	18 Edit Video	19 Reshoot and Edit Video	20 Post Video
23 Prep for Shooting	24 Shooting Day!	25 Edit Video	26 Reshoot and Edit Video	27 Post Video
30	1	2	3	4

Outline

Scripts aren't really necessary for video blogs. But having an outline of what you want to talk about will make your video shoots go more smoothly. You can list out all of the things you want to say or show during the course of the video.

An outline will also help you keep your thoughts together so you don't miss an important point. The last thing you want to do is have the camera rolling and not know what to do!

OUTLINE for the SHOOT

1. Introduction

2. Guest interview on frosting tips
   a) Cut to the recipe when the guest mentions it.

3. Show tools and ingredients.

4. Frosting the cupcakes

5. Adding bling to the frosting

6. Closing

1. introduction
2. Gest interview on frosting tips
a. cut to recipe when guest mentions
3. it show tools and ingredients
4. Frosting the cupcakes
5. Adding bling to the frosting
6. Closing

PRO TIP

Instead of writing your outline on a piece of paper, put it on a dry-erase board near the camera. That way, you can see what's next without looking down at a "cheat sheet."

Crew

Making a video blog is usually a solo adventure. There may be times, however, when it'll be helpful to have a crew assist with shooting the video. Ask your friends if they'd like to be a part of taking your video blog to the next level.

Members of your crew can do a number of different things. If you're blogging while walking, a friend could follow you with the camera. This will keep your hands free, letting you concentrate on what you're saying. Another friend can act as director to explain what should happen and where to put the camera.

PRO TIP

Getting help from a crew is great! Make sure you thank them by having water and snacks available for them during the shoot. Also, don't forget to include them in the credits for the vlog.

Backgrounds or Locations

Would you want to watch someone talk into the camera while sitting in front of the same boring wall day after day? Neither does your audience! A great background or location is a requirement for shooting your video.

PRO TIP

Try to find a space where you can control the light. This will make your videos look consistent if you shoot there again.

Pick a place that's interesting to look at. Maybe near a fireplace or a colorful bookshelf. Does your room have fun things in it? Shoot it in there. Just make sure you have permission to use the location you choose. If you choose a location that's not in your neighborhood, ask an adult to take you there.

Being on Camera

One of the hardest parts about video blogs is putting yourself in front of the camera. What if I look dumb? Will people think I sound funny? Don't worry! If you've got interesting things to talk about, you'll be fine.

A lot of video bloggers use weird voices or act crazy to get a lot of attention. While it might be funny at first, it can get old fast. Practice what you're going to say a few times and get ready for the spotlight!

PRO TIP

Consider having a guest on your video blog from time to time. Sometimes great content can be created by having someone to talk to. Anything you can do to keep your video interesting will keep viewers hooked.

Vlogging with a guest (or two) can be lots of fun! ☺ ☺ ☺

Practice Shoots

Do a practice shoot of your video ahead of time. Don't worry about making it perfect, but try filming yourself to test it out. Pretend you're doing the real thing and record a few minutes with just you talking to the camera.

When you're filming, it can be easy to get tongue-twisted. ☺

Practicing helps!

Watch the video and see if you have any nervous tics. Are you saying "uhh," "err," or any other words a lot? Are you talking too fast? Too slow? Are you clearing your throat over and over? Watching yourself is hard, but it can help you improve your presentation.

PRO TIP

Relax! The best thing you can do is be yourself on camera. Once you calm down and practice a few times, the nervousness should disappear.

Set It Up

You've got your outline ready. You have a good spot to shoot. You feel great about your topic and how you'll look on camera. You're even wearing your favorite T-shirt. It's time to set up your video shoot.

Position your camera and tripod so you're in the middle of the shot, with the lens just above your eyeline, but pointed down a little. You'll want to be about an arm's length away from the camera. If possible, ask someone to help you line up your shot. When you're all set, lock the tripod and don't let the camera move.

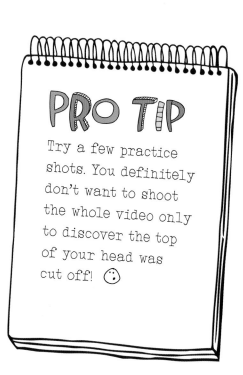

PRO TIP

Try a few practice shots. You definitely don't want to shoot the whole video only to discover the top of your head was cut off! :)

And ... Action!

At long last, you're ready to start filming for real! Hit record and start talking. Use your outline to help keep you focused. Do your best to look into the camera lens so it will appear you're talking directly to your viewers. Most important? Have fun!

Make a mistake or lose track of where you are? No problem. Go back to where you were and pick it up again. The great thing about video is that you can shoot a lot of footage. Even better, you can fix mistakes when you're editing.

PRO TIP

Resist the urge to play back every chunk of video you shoot right away. This will break up the rhythm of your video, and you'll end up reshooting more than you need to.

Shot Options

To keep your video interesting, you need some variety! Adjust the camera, film different things in the room, or film from different angles. Try this:

Pan and Tilt Shots—moving the camera from left to right (pan) or moving the camera up or down (tilt)

pan shot
(left to right)

tilt shot
(up or down)

PRO TIP

While variety is good, moving the camera around too much and adding too many crazy shots can be a bit distracting. You still want your viewers to understand what you're talking about.

Exterior Shot—filming the location where video is taking place; if you're filming in an apartment, shoot a bit of the outside of the building; exterior shots help your audience get a clear sense of the location

Close-Up—getting up close and personal to the person, object, or place you're filming

Zoom—using the built-in zoom feature to move closer to (zoom in) or farther away from (zoom out) the object you're filming; this is sometimes a sliding bar or a button on a digital camera

wide-angle
(pull camera back)

Wide-Angle—pulling the camera back so that more of the scene is shown

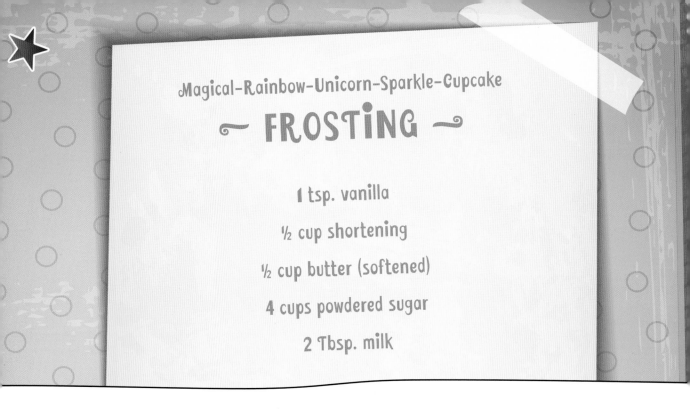

Magical-Rainbow-Unicorn-Sparkle-Cupcake
~ FROSTING ~

1 tsp. vanilla

½ cup shortening

½ cup butter (softened)

4 cups powdered sugar

2 Tbsp. milk

Cutaways

It's always good to get more footage than you'll need. Did your cat come into the room? Film her! Does your stuffed bear have a goofy look on its face? Capture it!

PRO TIP

You sneezed while talking? Keep it. Throwing that little cutaway in can actually be comedy gold! Learn to laugh at yourself, and your viewers will see you've got a sense of humor.

Cutaways are great ways to give your audience a break. Sure, they'll love to watch *you*, but cutting away to something else, even for a second, keeps your vlog fun and interesting. The more cutaways you have to choose from, the happier you'll be when it's time to edit.

Playback

You've filmed everything you wanted to talk about. You went through your entire outline. It's all sitting in your camera, waiting for you to take a look! Grab a notebook and a pencil and watch your footage.

Make notes about what you're seeing. Is there a long pause where nothing is happening? Write that down. Miss something? Remind yourself to film another quick clip to stick in there.

PRO TIP

Ask a friend to take a look at the footage with you and make notes for edits. Getting a second opinion is always helpful!

PLAYBACK NOTES

1. I stumbled with my wording in the second shot.

2. I forgot to mention a step in making the frosting.

3. My voice was too low at the end of the fifth shot.

4. Reshoot the close-ups of the cupcakes.

Editing

OK, time to edit! Editing is like assembling a puzzle. The nice thing about vlogs is that the pieces are usually all shot in order. Putting them together is a snap!

Pull all of your video footage into the editing app/software. (Check page 48 for suggested editing programs.) With your handy edit notes, cut out the pieces you don't want. Pull in some of the cutaways you added. Consult your outline to make sure it's all there.

PRO TIP

Never permanently delete the footage you're not using. Hold onto it. You never know when mistakes or alternate shots might come in handy.

Rough Cut

The new version of your edited video is what's known as a "rough cut." It has all the pieces put together in the order you want. It should make sense when you watch it from beginning to end.

Play through it and look for other tweaks you might want to make. The best rule of thumb is to keep it short and sweet. Cut out any coughs, pauses, or breaks in the action. Pacing is how well a scene works by keeping things moving. If what's happening on screen seems slow or dull to you, your audience will think so too. A video with good pacing will keep your audience engaged!

♡ Keep this!

And then jump to a close-up of the sparkles.

☒ Cut some of the mixing time. It's too long.

PRO TIP

Most new video bloggers should try to keep their videos around two minutes or less. It'll be hard to get someone to sit through a video that's 10 to 15 minutes long.

Intro ☆ Logo

One thing you'll notice with video bloggers who have been around awhile is their intro. An intro is like the opening credits of a TV show. A video blogger might even have a name for his vlog, like "TV Talk with DJ Dustin".

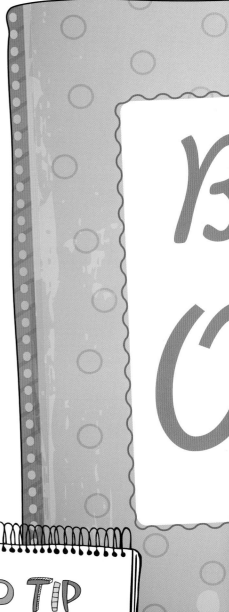

If you decide you want to keep making video blogs, think of a name for it. Consider drawing or making a logo to "brand" your vlog. That will make it stand out from the rest of the video blogs out there. Thinking about sharing your video blog on the internet? Ask an adult to help you tag your video and give it a good description. Tagging will help viewers interested in your topic find your vlog.

Let's say your vlog is about TV shows. Tag examples:
☆ TV
☆ Reviews
☆ TV Talk with DJ Dustin

PRO TIP

Once you have a bunch of video blogs made, you can assemble a quick little intro using "best of" clips from each. It'll give new viewers a quick taste of what your vlog is about.

aking with

livia

Music and Visual Effects

Now that you've got your video edited down to where you want it, ask yourself: Is it missing anything else? Consider adding some background music. Music can add another level to your video. Just make sure you don't have the music so loud it drowns out your voice.

Many editing applications have visual effects built in. You can have words pop up for emphasis. You can change the video image from color to black and white. While video effects can be fun, overdoing it can be distracting.

Be sure to use music you have permission to use! You can find a lot of "free to use" music on the internet. Just make sure an adult helps you download it.

Rainbow-Unicorn-Sparkle-Cupcake
FROSTING

Video Blog Vanguard!

After all of your great ideas and hard work, your video blog is done! Time to share it with your friends and family. Have a viewing party so they can see what your vlog is all about. Chances are, they'll think it's great and will be hungry for your next one! Want to see if people around the world will watch it? Make sure anyone appearing in the video has given you permission to post it.

Then see if your parents/guardians are OK with you uploading it to the internet (YouTube, Vimeo).

Making great video blogs can take some trial and error. With a little practice, finding your voice and style will become as easy as riding a bike. It's fun to become a video blog star. Not only will you be able to share subjects and topics with your friends and family, you might end up finding a larger audience and reaching people all over the world!

PRO TIP

If you don't want to use your real name (or other identifying information), be sure to remove it from the video before posting it online.

Meet Your Film Instructor

Thomas Kingsley Troupe is an amateur filmmaker who has been making goofy movies and videos since he was in high school. Thomas has worked in the visual effects department for a handful of Hollywood movies and shows. He has also written and directed a number of short films for the 48 Hour Film Fest & Z Fest contests and loves creating funny videos with his own sons at home. Thomas says, "Making movies is the BEST. It can be a lot of work, but finishing a movie to show to your friends and family is WORTH IT!"

Read More

Grabham, Tim. *Video Ideas.* New York: DK publishing, 2018.

Juilly, Brett. *Make Your Own Amazing YouTube Videos.* New York: Racehorse for Young Readers, 2017.

Internet Sites

National Geographic Kids: Photo Tips and Tricks
https://kids.nationalgeographic.com/explore/tips-tricks/

Glossary

app—a computer application

blog—a regular feature appearing as part of an online publication that typically relates to a particular topic and consists of articles and personal commentary by one or more authors

consistent—always looking or behaving the same

director—the person who is in charge of a show

edit—to cut and rearrange pieces of film to make a movie or TV program

footage—the total number of running feet for a film

rough cut—the first version of a movie after early editing

script—the story for a play, movie, video blog, or TV show

vanguard—the forefront of a movement or action

webcam—a camera used for transmitting live images over the Internet

Apps and Software

iMovie, by Apple—an app to create beautiful movies

Movie Maker Movavi Clips, by Movavi Software, Inc.—an advanced video-making app for your smartphone

Movie Maker 10, by Microsoft—a full movie-making software for all budding artists

Index